Robot Rampage

Chris Priestley ■ Jonatronix

THUD, THUD, THUD.

The monster started to hammer at the buildings on either side of the alleyway. Bricks and dust flew in all directions.

"It's coming!" cried Cat.

THUD, THUD, THUD.

There was a huge rumbling crash as one wall was destroyed.

All four children started screaming.

Chapter 1 – Earlier that day …

"Come on," called out Tiger. "We're going to be late."

"I'm trying," shouted Max, as he struggled to get past a woman with a pram.

Cat and Ant were even further behind. They were heading towards the cinema. It was the opening day of the new Robo-Rex II film, *Robot Rampage,* and they wanted to be the first to see it. The only trouble was that everyone else on the crowded pavement seemed to be going in the opposite direction.

"This way," said Tiger, turning sharp left. "Short cut," he explained.

Tiger was a huge Robo-Rex fan. It had taken him ages to save up enough pocket money to buy a remote-controlled Robo-Rex II. It was his favourite toy. He had even brought it with him. Now he had the chance to see Robo-Rex on the big screen – in 3D! He had barely talked about anything else for weeks. He was determined not to miss it.

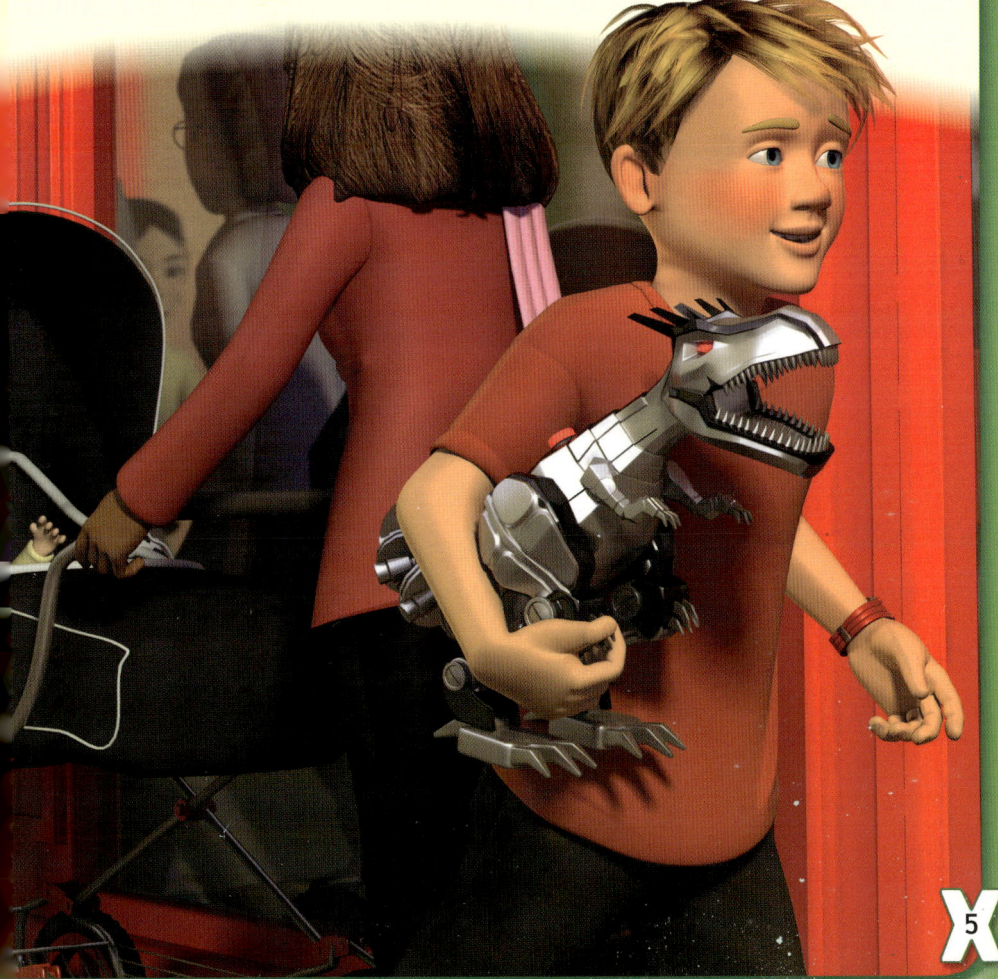

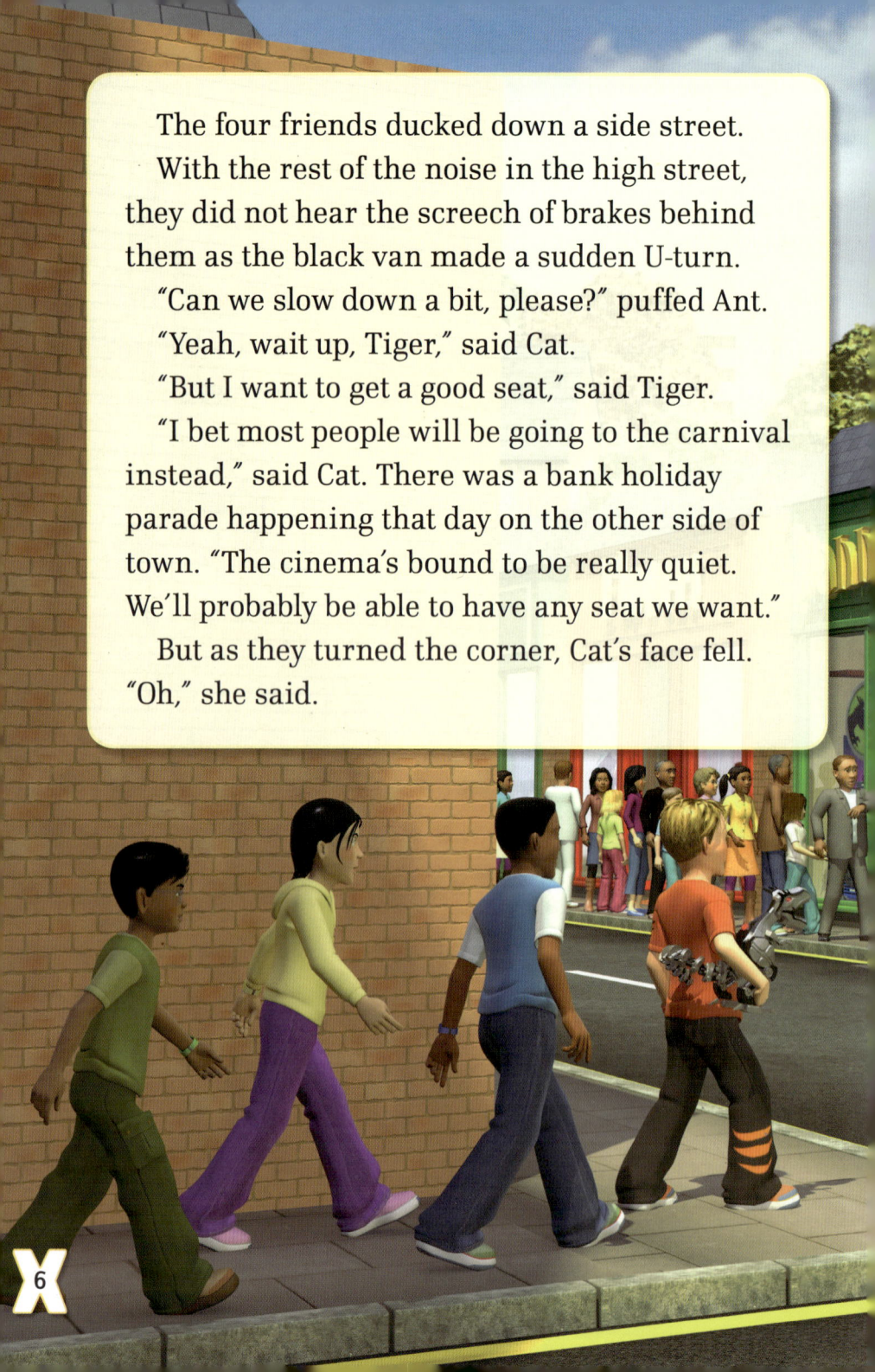

The four friends ducked down a side street.
With the rest of the noise in the high street, they did not hear the screech of brakes behind them as the black van made a sudden U-turn.

"Can we slow down a bit, please?" puffed Ant.

"Yeah, wait up, Tiger," said Cat.

"But I want to get a good seat," said Tiger.

"I bet most people will be going to the carnival instead," said Cat. There was a bank holiday parade happening that day on the other side of town. "The cinema's bound to be really quiet. We'll probably be able to have any seat we want."

But as they turned the corner, Cat's face fell. "Oh," she said.

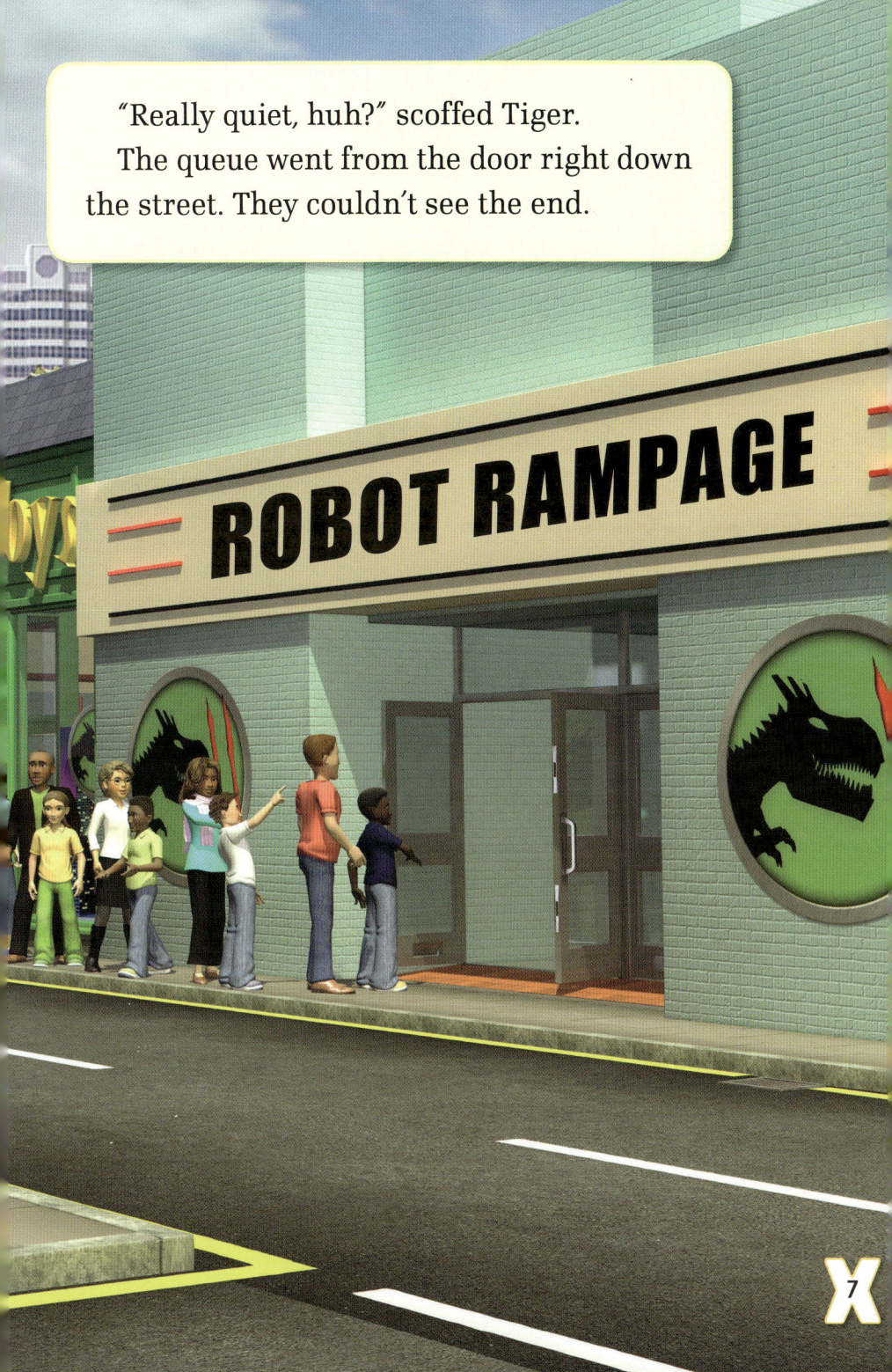

"Really quiet, huh?" scoffed Tiger.
The queue went from the door right down the street. They couldn't see the end.

Chapter 2 – The black van

Tiger pushed the button on the remote control and Robo-Rex's long tail swished to one side.

"You're wasting the batteries," said Cat.

"Don't care," said Tiger miserably. They had been queuing for over twenty minutes. "We'll never get a seat at this rate." He pushed the button again.

"Ow!" said Ant, as the tail hit him in the ribs.

"Hey," said Max, "I think the queue is moving." He shuffled forwards one place. "Yes, it's definitely moving."

Finally, the children reached the front of the queue.

The street was almost deserted now, except for the black van parked near the cinema.

"Has anyone noticed that van over there?" said Cat, who had been watching it for some time.

"What about it?" asked Max.

"Well, it just seems a bit odd. It arrived just after we did ... and no one's got out yet."

"It's probably nothing, Cat," said Max. "Come on, you don't want to miss the start."

Cat shrugged and jogged up the steps after the others.

After they had gone, a hand appeared at the window of the van. It was holding a remote control. A soft chuckling started up from inside the van. At first it was just one voice, but then another joined in and then another. The chuckling grew louder until the van rumbled with the sound of laughter.

Chapter 3 - Robo-Rex vs Metallix

The children's eyes took a moment to adjust to the gloom after coming in from the brightly lit foyer. The film was being shown on Screen 1, the biggest screen. But there were only four seats left, right at the front.

"We're going to get neck ache," complained Cat. She had to lean back in her seat just to see the screen.

"I don't care," said Tiger. He was grinning so much his face hurt.

The children put on their 3D glasses as the lights started to dim.

"This is going to be great!" said Max excitedly.

"Ssshhhhh!" hissed a woman behind them.

"Sorry," said Max, blushing.

Suddenly there was a giant roar. Cat jumped, spilling her popcorn over Ant.

On-screen, a meteorite shot forwards ... it looked as if it was coming right out of the screen. The meteorite crashed to Earth. It cracked open and Metallix, a giant monster robot, stomped out. It had been sent by evil warlords from another planet. It looked like the Earth was doomed. Robo-Rex II was about to face his biggest challenge yet ...

The lights flickering off the screen gave the cinema an eerie glow. But the children did not notice. The film was just reaching a good bit. Robo-Rex and Metallix had just met. Sparks flew as they fought each other. The sound blasted out from the speakers making the children flinch every time a blow was struck.

"Careful, Robo-Rex!" Tiger yelped.

"Ssshhhhh!" hissed the woman behind them, even more loudly this time.

Tiger was concentrating so hard on the film that he did not hear her. Neither did he notice his watch beginning to flash.

Cat did, however. As she took a handful of popcorn, she glanced down and saw the familiar red warning signal on Tiger's watch.

"X-bots!" gasped Cat.

"Don't be silly," whispered Tiger, still staring at the screen. "It's Metallix!"

"No, Tiger. Your watch ... look!"

Tiger had to drag his eyes away from the screen.

"Not now!" he moaned.

"Maybe the film projector equipment is making your watch go wrong?" Max suggested.

"I doubt it," said Ant.

"If you lot don't be quiet," hissed the woman behind them, "I'll have you thrown –"

But she didn't finish her sentence because at that moment a huge, black, metallic head burst through the screen with a ripping sound. Its eyes glowed a horrible red in the darkened auditorium.

Chapter 4 - Trapped

"That's no special effect!" said Cat.

"A giant X-bot!" gasped Max. "Run!"

Max, Cat and Ant jumped out of their seats, but Tiger was frozen. Cat picked up his Robo-Rex toy and shoved it at him.

"Come *on*!" she yelled.

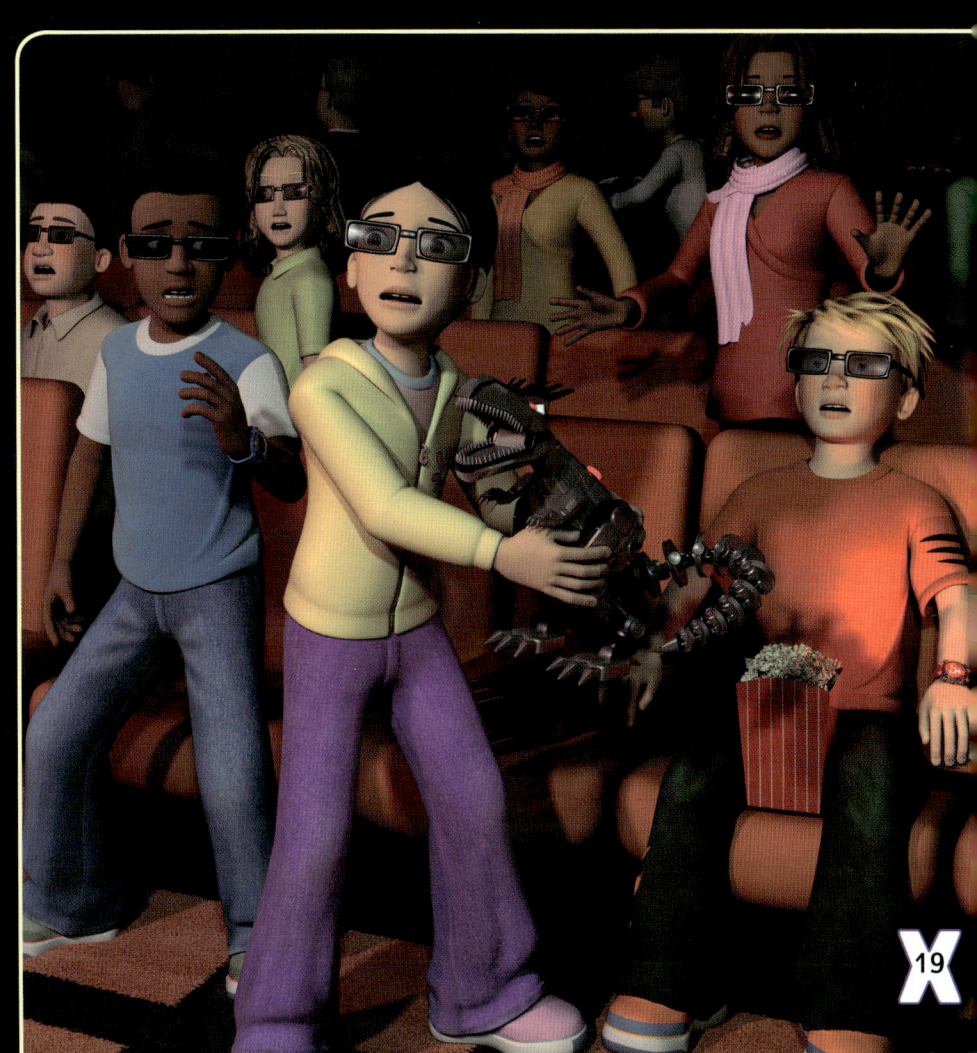

Tiger shook himself and leapt to his feet. He ran after the others.

It was chaos outside. People were streaming out of the other cinema screens, and the staff were shouting and trying to find out what was going on.

Max, Cat, Ant and Tiger were caught in the crowd pushing its way outside. Once out of the cinema, they fought their way free of the crowd. They looked up as a shadow fell over them.

Standing in front of them was an enormous X-bot, the sleek, black metal of its body glinting in the sun. Its huge head creaked as it moved back and forth.

The X-bot had stopped its attack on the cinema. It was standing at its full height, towering above the street, just like Metallix had done in the film. People ran about like ants beneath it.

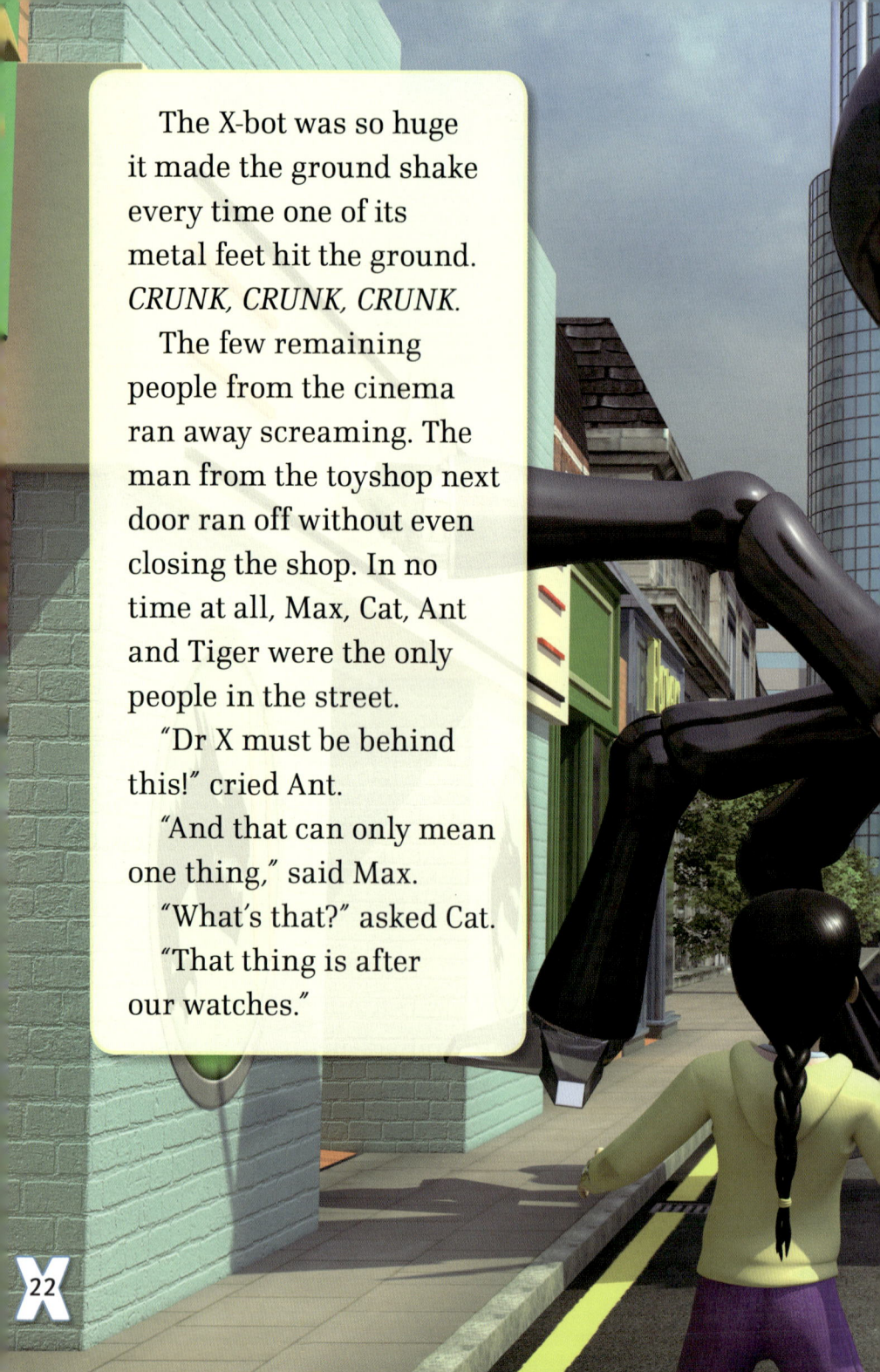

The X-bot was so huge it made the ground shake every time one of its metal feet hit the ground. *CRUNK, CRUNK, CRUNK.*

The few remaining people from the cinema ran away screaming. The man from the toyshop next door ran off without even closing the shop. In no time at all, Max, Cat, Ant and Tiger were the only people in the street.

"Dr X must be behind this!" cried Ant.

"And that can only mean one thing," said Max.

"What's that?" asked Cat.

"That thing is after our watches."

Just at that moment, the X-bot turned its huge head and looked down at them. Its neck made a grating metallic sound as it turned. The light flickered in its eyes, and it started to move towards them. *CRUNK, CRUNK, CRUNK.*

"Let's get out of here!" yelled Max.

The children ran, not daring to look back. They could hear the monster X-bot behind them. The ground shook with every step it took.

"Down here!" said Max, ducking into a side street.

The street was narrow with tall buildings on either side. The X-bot was too big to fit down it.

The X-bot swiped at them with one of its front feet, like a cat trying to get a mouse out of a hole. Its foot whistled past their heads, only just missing them.

It gnashed its jaws together. Then it made a metallic hissing noise. It sounded a lot like a chuckle.

"Uh-oh," said Ant.

He had noticed the same thing the X-bot had noticed. The alley was a dead end. There were high brick walls hemming them in and only one door. But when Cat tried it she found it was locked. The X-bot might not be able to get in, but the children could not get out either.

THUD, THUD, THUD.

The monster started to hammer at the buildings on either side of the alleyway. Bricks and dust flew in all directions.

"It's coming!" cried Cat.

THUD, THUD, THUD.

There was a huge rumbling crash as one wall was destroyed.

All four children started screaming.

Chapter 5 - Tiger's plan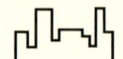

The brick walls of the alleyway stretched above them, with only a window of sky above. The only other opening was filled with the X-bot smashing its way towards the four helpless friends.

"What are we going to do?" said Cat. "We're trapped!"

"I ... don't know," said Max. For once he was out of ideas.

Tiger was still holding his Robo-Rex toy. It had been awkward to carry when he had been running, and he had thought about dropping it. But even as he had the thought, he had clutched on to Robo-Rex more tightly. He was not just going to abandon his favourite toy. Now it gave him an idea ...

Tiger thrust Robo-Rex at Max. "Hold this," he said, looking round the alley. "We're not beaten yet."

"You've got a plan?" said Ant hopefully. He glanced at the massive X-bot getting nearer and nearer.

Tiger ignored the question. He had just spotted a broken drainpipe. "Perfect!" He ran over to it, held his hands under it and collected a large handful of water.

Then he threw it over Ant.

"Argh!" yelled Ant. "That's not my idea of a plan!"
"Yeah," said Cat. "What are you doing, Tiger?"
Tiger began to stare at Ant's watch.
"Hey, Tiger!" shouted Ant, again.
"Remember what happens when your watch gets wet?" Tiger said to Ant. "It grows things! Remember the chicken? Your hamster?"

"You want to grow Robo-Rex?" gasped Cat.

"Genius!" said Max.

"You could have just asked me to put my watch in the water," said Ant, still dripping.

"Hmmm," said Tiger, "I never thought of ... Hey, it's working!"

Just at that moment there was a fizzing noise from Ant's watch.

Max quickly put Robo-Rex on the ground. A bolt of green light flashed out from Ant's watch and hit Robo-Rex. Robo-Rex began to grow ... and grow ... and grow.

Chapter 6 – Robo-Rex vs X-bot

Robo-Rex made a creaking and stretching noise as it grew. It kept on growing until it was as tall as the buildings that overlooked the alley ... until it was as tall as the X-bot.

"Cool!" said Ant, craning his neck to look up. He had forgotten all about being wet.

The X-bot had stopped smashing its way towards the children. Now it was glaring at the giant Robo-Rex.

Tiger pulled the remote control out of his pocket.

Tiger pushed a button. Robo-Rex opened its huge mouth and let out a deafening and fearsome roar. The X-bot hissed back.

"Time to deal with that X-bot," said Tiger. He pushed the controls and made Robo-Rex step over the bricks and rubble knocked down by the X-bot.

Tiger's face was full of concentration as he controlled Robo-Rex and sent it towards the X-bot. The children followed Robo-Rex out of the alley.

The X-bot took a step back when it saw Robo-Rex coming. It let out a horrible metallic growl and gnashed its metal jaws. Robo-Rex swished its tail.

"Go get him, Robo-Rex!" shouted Tiger, pushing the controls.

"Go get him, Tiger!" shouted Max.

Robo-Rex stomped forwards …

Robo-Rex snapped its massive jaws round the X-bot's neck. The X-bot grabbed Robo-Rex with its front feet and began to squeeze.

They tugged and pushed each other, going round and round as they did so, each one looking for a chance to overpower the other. Every time Robo-Rex turned, its huge tail went whizzing over the children's heads.

"Watch what you're doing with that tail, Tiger!" shouted Cat.

But Tiger was finding it harder to work the controls than he thought he would.

Every time Tiger tried a new move, the X-bot always managed to get out of the way in the nick of time.

"Come on, Tiger," shouted Cat, above the din.

"I'm trying my best," he replied. "Think you can do any better?"

Cat held up her hands as Tiger shoved the remote towards her.

"No, no," she said. "I'm not doing it."

Just then, the X-bot saw its chance. While Tiger was distracted, it leapt forward and grabbed Robo-Rex, hurling him to the ground like a professional wrestler. Robo-Rex hit the floor with so much force that every car alarm in the street went off.

Tiger jabbed the buttons on the remote control, but nothing happened. Robo-Rex just lay there in a cloud of dust, refusing to budge. Then they saw that the red light had gone out in Robo-Rex's eyes.

X3
N.A.S.T.I.

"The batteries must have gone flat!" shouted Tiger, tears of frustration welling in his eyes.

"I told you you'd wear them ouuuuut," said Cat. Her last word was sucked up into the air as the X-bot reached down and grabbed her.

The boys watched helplessly as the X-bot carried Cat off down the street.

"Help!" yelled Cat.

The X-bot stomped noisily away on five of its legs. With the sixth, it held Cat aloft like a trophy. The boys set off in pursuit.

The X-bot was slow but it covered a lot of ground with each huge step. It was hard work trying to keep up.

"Where's it going?" puffed Ant.

But the answer became all too obvious as the X-bot reached the foot of the NICE building.

"NASTI," hissed Tiger.

With one look over its shoulder at the pursuing children, the X-bot started to climb up the outside of the tower.

"Oh, no!" said Max, looking up.

The dome at the top of the building began to open up, ready to receive the monster X-bot ... and its prize.

N.I.C.E.

Meanwhile ...

The figures in the black van watched the monster X-bot climb up the side of the building. The laughter started again.

N.I.C.E.

To be continued ...

Find out what happens next ...

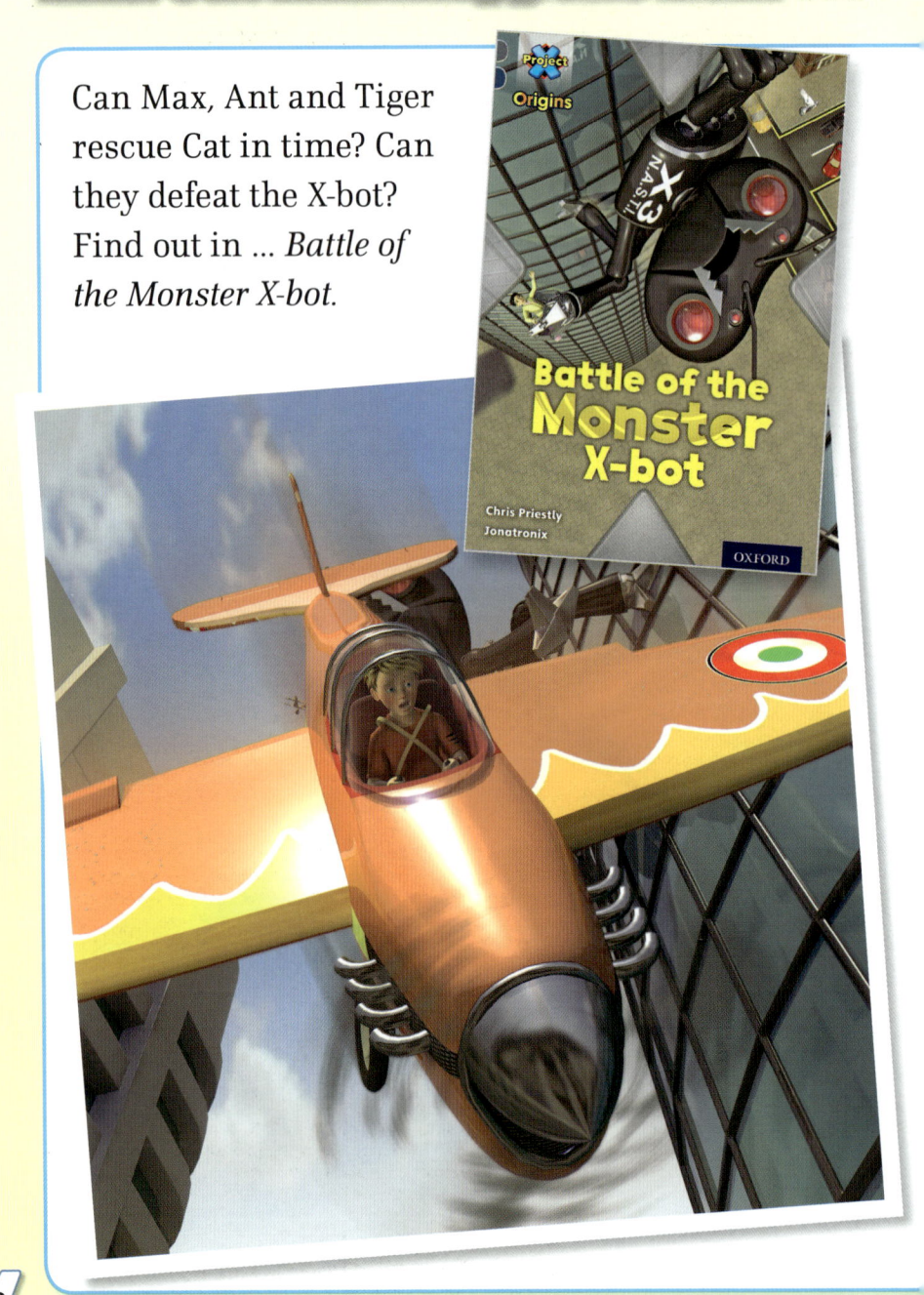

Can Max, Ant and Tiger rescue Cat in time? Can they defeat the X-bot? Find out in ... *Battle of the Monster X-bot.*